To

From

Date

A Bible Story About Rahab

AN UNEXPECTED
HERO

RACHEL SPIER WEAVER | **ANNA HAGGARD**

Illustrated by **ERIC ELWELL**

HARVEST HOUSE PUBLISHERS
EUGENE, OREGON

An Unexpected Hero

Text © 2019 by Rachel Spier Weaver and Anna Haggard
Artwork © 2019 by Eric Elwell

Published by Harvest House Publishers
Eugene, Oregon 97408

www.harvesthousepublishers.com

Published in association with the literary agency of Wolgemuth & Associates, Inc.

Cover and interior design by Left Coast Design

HARVEST KIDS is a trademark of The Hawkins Children's LLC. Harvest House Publishers, Inc., is the exclusive licensee of the trademark HARVEST KIDS.

ISBN 978-0-7369-7373-1 (hardcover)

Library of Congress Cataloging-in-Publication Data

Names: Weaver, Rachel Spier, author. | Haggard, Anna, author. | Elwell, Eric, illustrator.
Title: An unexpected hero : a Bible story about Rahab / Rachel Spier Weaver
   and Anna Haggard ; illustrated by Eric Elwell.
Description: Eugene, Oregon : Harvest House Publishers, [2018]
Identifiers: LCCN 2018013036 (print) | LCCN 2018020749 (ebook) | ISBN
   9780736973748 (ebook) | ISBN 9780736973731 (hardcover)
Subjects: LCSH: Rahab (Biblical figure)—Juvenile literature.
Classification: LCC BS580.R3 (ebook) | LCC BS580.R3 W43 2018 (print) | DDC
   222/.2092—dc23
LC record available at https://lccn.loc.gov/2018013036

Printed in China

19 20 21 22 23 24 25 26 27 / LP / 10 9 8 7 6 5 4 3 2 1

Rahab's Story

Joshua 2; 6
Matthew 1:5
Hebrews 11:31
James 2:25

Based on the story found in the Old Testament,
An Unexpected Hero follows the biblical narrative
of the heroine Rahab, imagining how she responded
to the events recorded in Scripture.

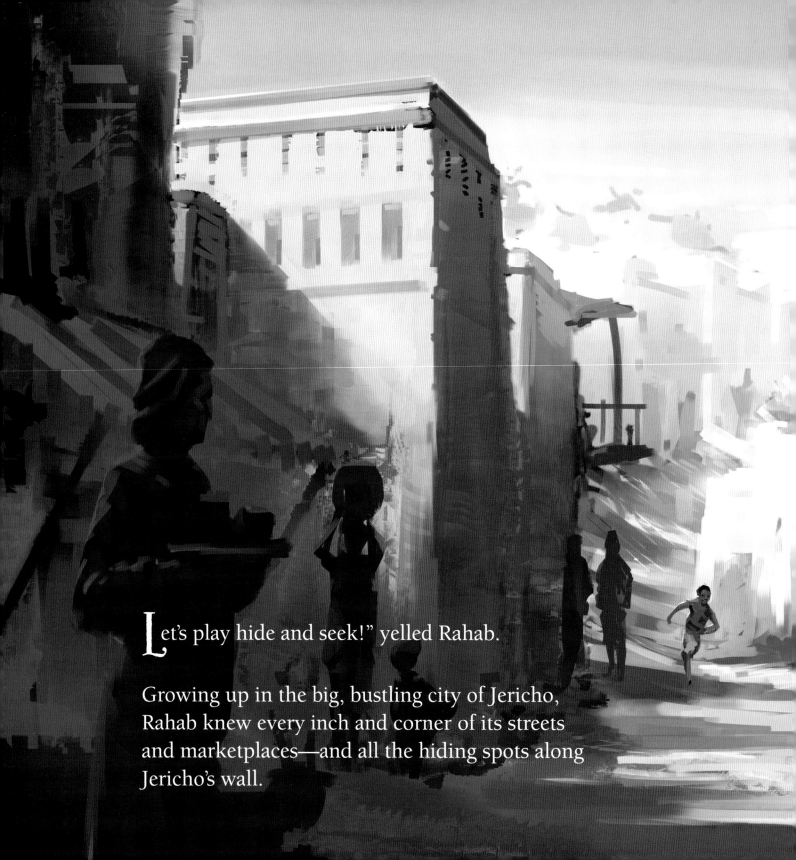

"Let's play hide and seek!" yelled Rahab.

Growing up in the big, bustling city of Jericho, Rahab knew every inch and corner of its streets and marketplaces—and all the hiding spots along Jericho's wall.

"You're it," she said, tagging her eldest brother. Grabbing her little sister's hand, Rahab rushed with her sister through the city streets to find a hiding spot.

Suddenly, Rahab saw a small, tight space in the wall! Only one person could fit. Should Rahab take it or give it to her sister?

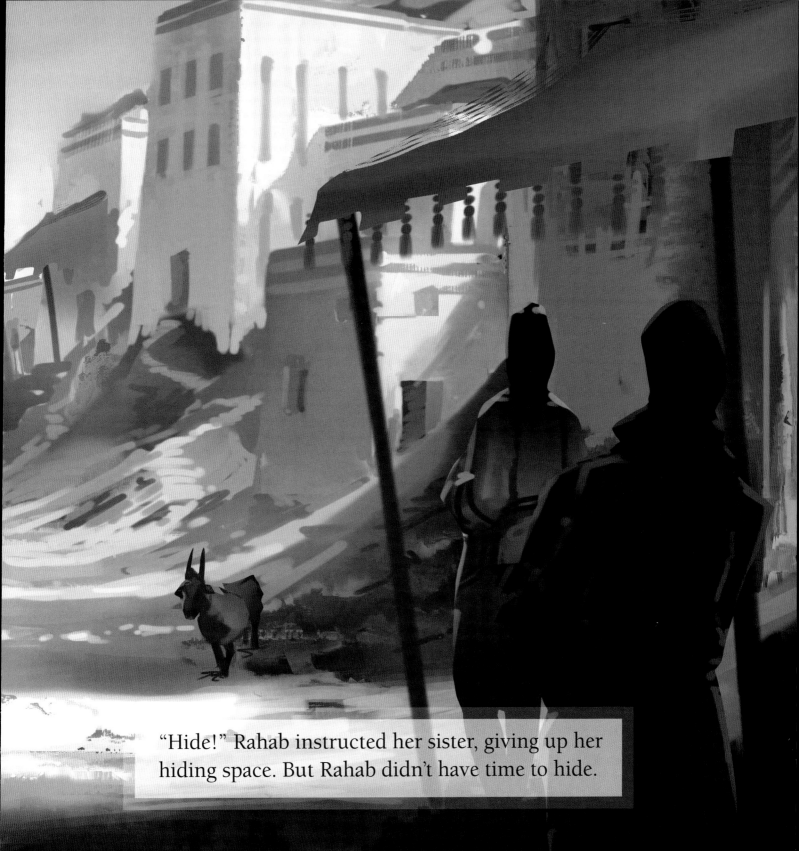

"Hide!" Rahab instructed her sister, giving up her hiding space. But Rahab didn't have time to hide.

"Got you!" said her oldest brother. With eyes gleaming, he asked, "Now, where's our sister?"

Rahab would never tell where her sister was hiding—she always protected her siblings.

As she grew up, Rahab began spending time with people who didn't love her and who treated her poorly. She made a lot of bad choices.

Rahab wanted desperately to change her life.

One day, from her home deep in the city wall, Rahab spotted two young travelers.

"They look like Israelites," she said.

Everyone in Jericho was talking about the people of Israel. Their God loved them and did mighty miracles, like parting the Red Sea and leading them to a new land.

Rahab wondered, *Could the God of the Israelites love me too?*

Suddenly, the two men were at her door! She peeked out. "Tell me honestly—are you Israelites?" she asked.

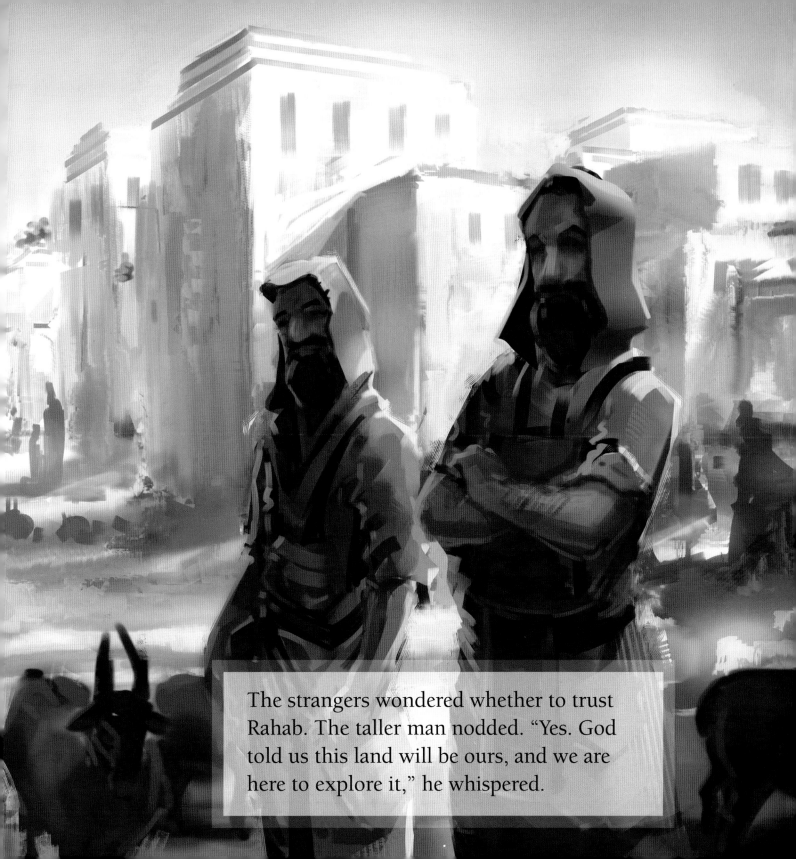

The strangers wondered whether to trust Rahab. The taller man nodded. "Yes. God told us this land will be ours, and we are here to explore it," he whispered.

Rahab knew the king of Jericho would not be pleased the Israelites were staying in the city, and he would want to capture them.

Taking a deep breath, Rahab
made a big decision, one that
would change her life.

"Come quickly." Rahab pulled them into the house. She scanned the room for places to hide. Behind water jars? Under blankets piled for sleeping? In the storage room?

Then she spied the ladder to the roof.

No one will look there! Rahab thought. She led the spies through the roof's trapdoor and hid them under flax laid out to dry.

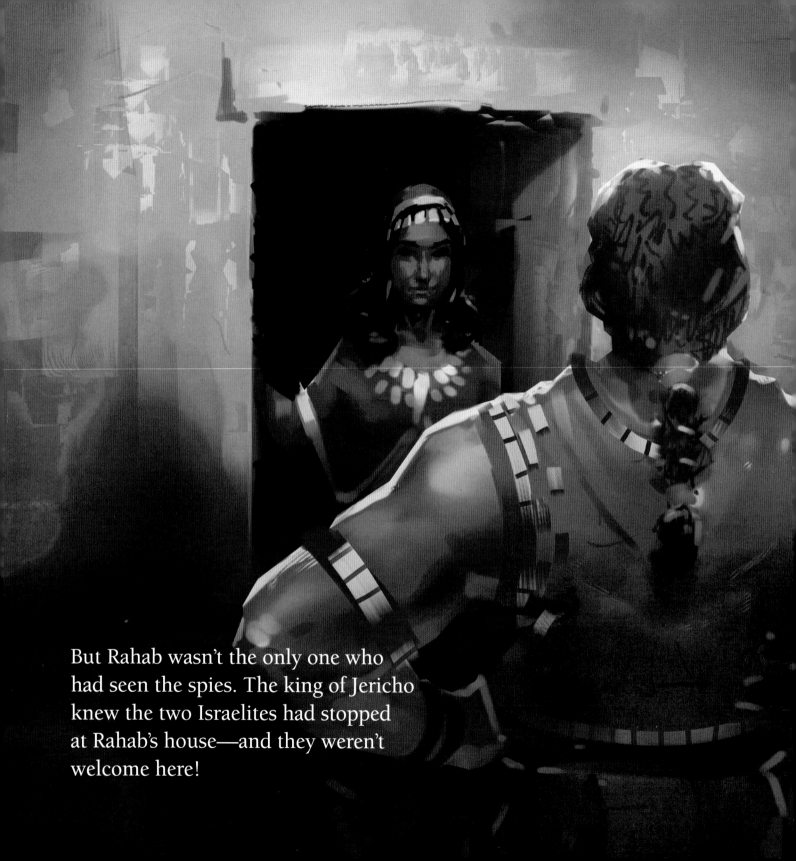

But Rahab wasn't the only one who had seen the spies. The king of Jericho knew the two Israelites had stopped at Rahab's house—and they weren't welcome here!

The king sent his messenger to Rahab's door. "Where are the two men who entered your home?" the king's messenger bellowed.

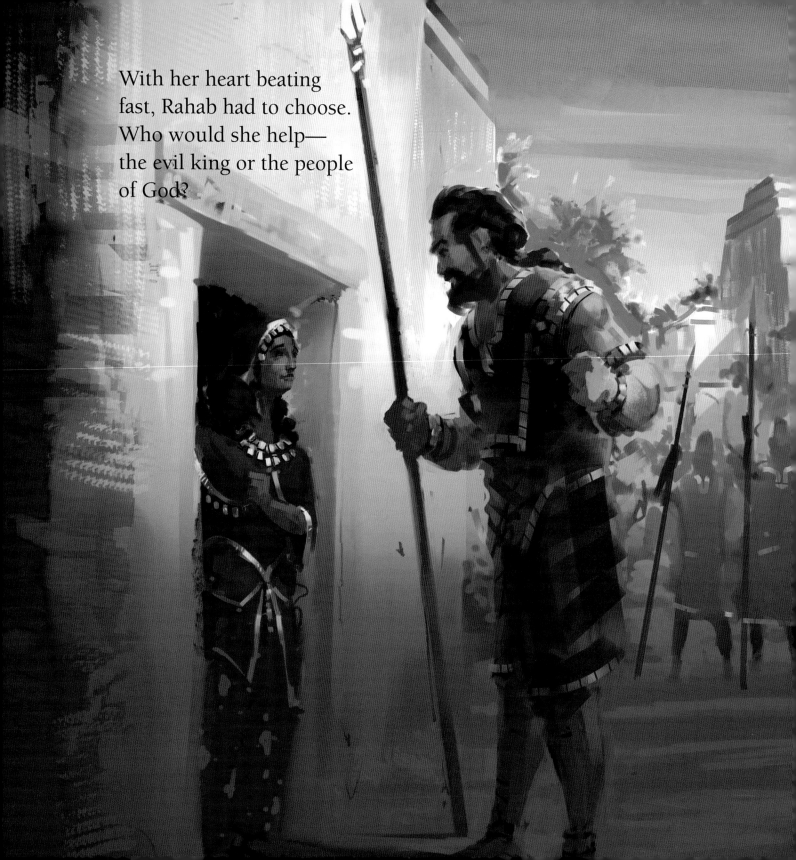

With her heart beating
fast, Rahab had to choose.
Who would she help—
the evil king or the people
of God?

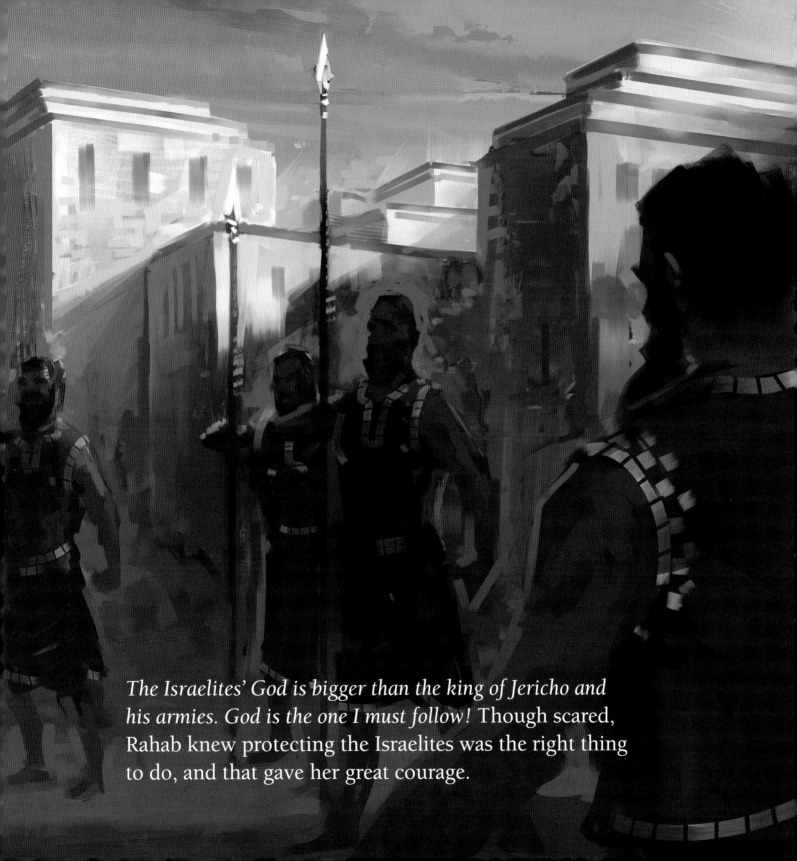

The Israelites' God is bigger than the king of Jericho and his armies. God is the one I must follow! Though scared, Rahab knew protecting the Israelites was the right thing to do, and that gave her great courage.

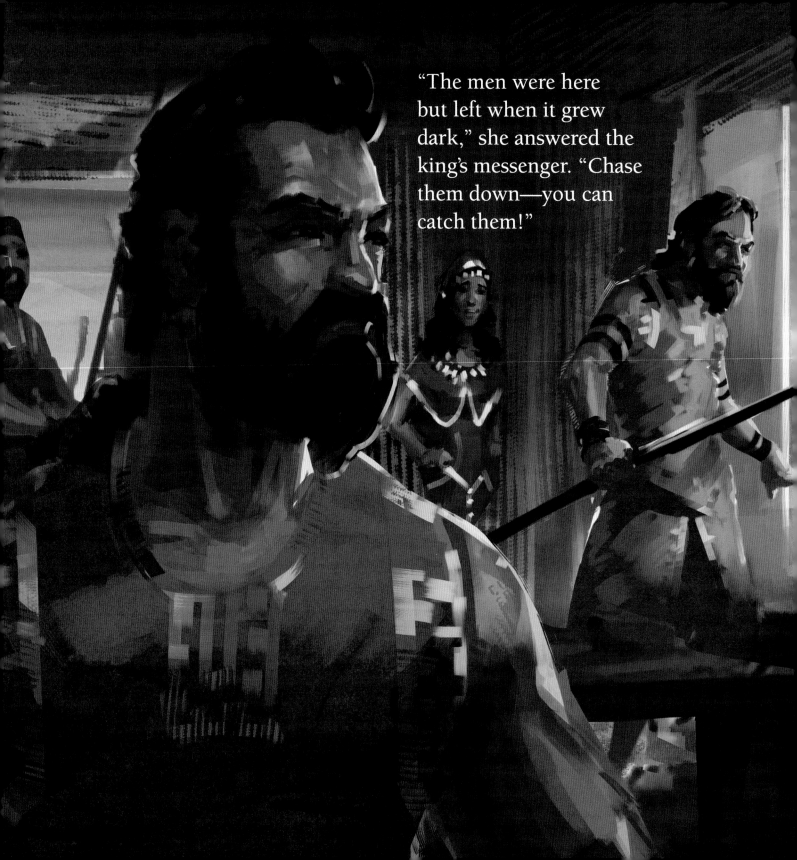

"The men were here but left when it grew dark," she answered the king's messenger. "Chase them down—you can catch them!"

Following winding streets, the messenger and his troops ran out of the city in search of the two men.

Clang! The king shut the city gate after the troops. The only way to enter or leave Jericho was through that gate. The spies were trapped inside Jericho!

Though Rahab didn't know the God of the Israelites, she needed help. Would God listen to Rahab?

She began to pray. "God, I know you're real;
help me break these two men free from
Jericho's great wall!"

And God listened to Rahab! Suddenly, in the corner of the room, she noticed a red rope. She had an idea!

Grabbing the coil of
rope, she climbed the
ladder to the roof, where
the men were hiding.

"The king of Jericho has barred the gate, and you're locked in the city," she said quickly. "But your God is bigger than the king and has given me a plan."

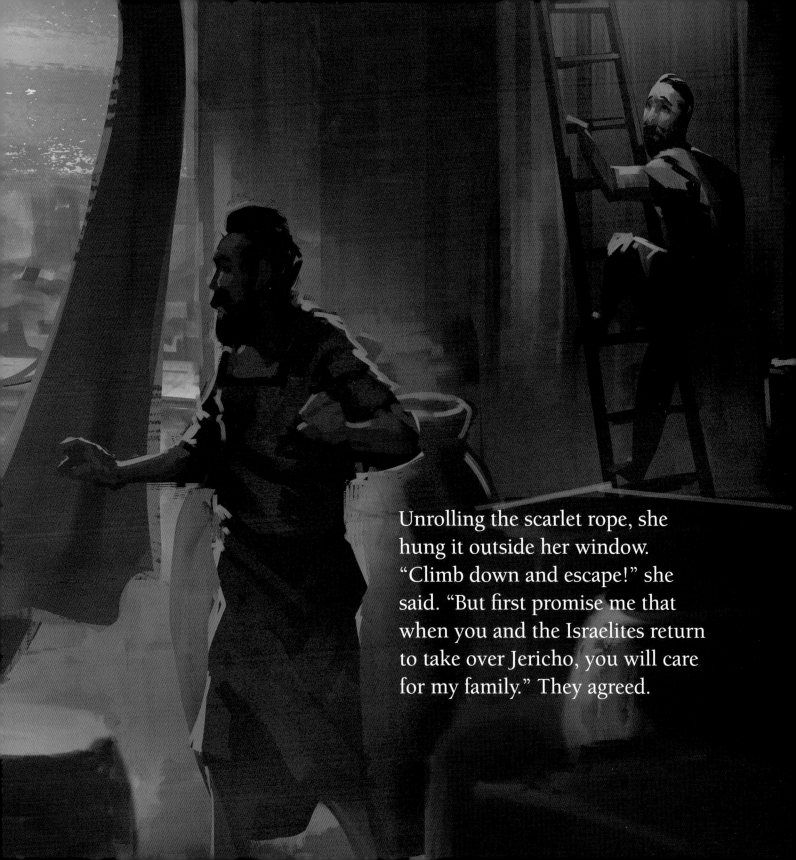

Unrolling the scarlet rope, she hung it outside her window. "Climb down and escape!" she said. "But first promise me that when you and the Israelites return to take over Jericho, you will care for my family." They agreed.

"Keep this rope in the window," the spies said. "That way, we will recognize your house, and your family will be saved."

And with that, they were gone.

Sometime later, the Israelite army surrounded the
city of Jericho. They marched around its
thick wall once a day for six days.

On the seventh day, God told the Israelites to march around the city seven times. During the seventh time, they blew horns and shouted at the top of their lungs!

Inside the wall, Rahab covered her ears.

The noise was so loud.

CRACK!
POP!

The God of the Israelites was causing the city's wall to fall! As the wall collapsed around them, Rahab and her family ducked in a corner.

Silence came over the household.

The candles had blown out—it was black.

How would anyone find Rahab and her family now?

Would God remember Rahab?

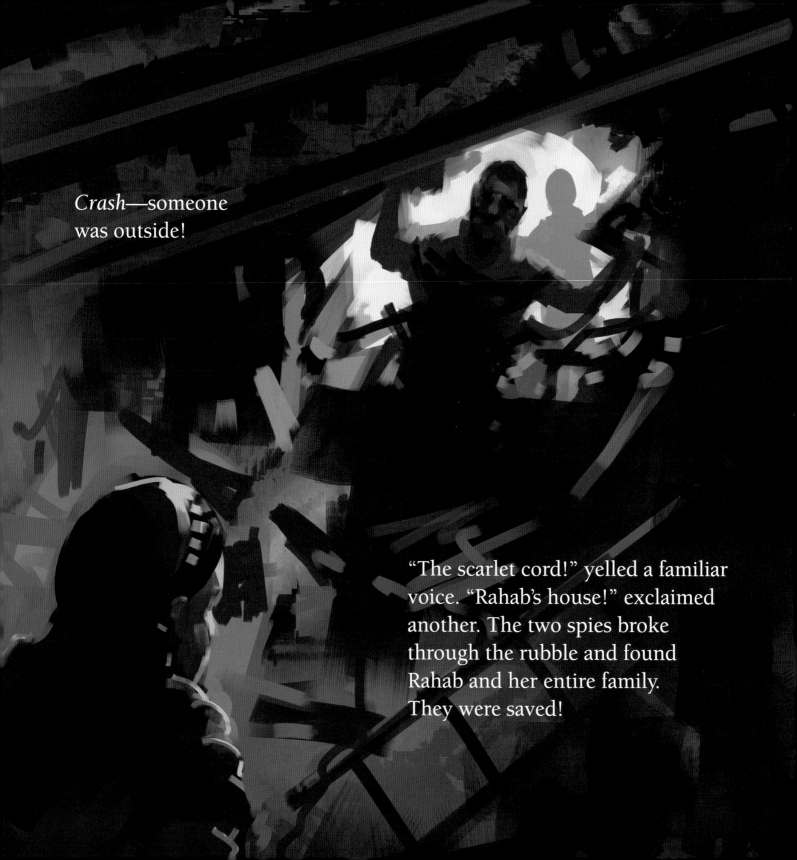

Crash—someone was outside!

"The scarlet cord!" yelled a familiar voice. "Rahab's house!" exclaimed another. The two spies broke through the rubble and found Rahab and her entire family. They were saved!

Climbing through the wreckage, Rahab was greeted by the leaders of the Israelite people. "We heard how your courage saved two of our spies. Because of your bravery, *your* family is now part of *our* family."

Rahab cried with joy. God had given her a new home, a new people—a new beginning! Most of all, Rahab had risked everything to believe in the God of the Israelites. And she had discovered God *loved* her too!

Because of her courage, God made Rahab a part of the greatest story on Earth: She became the great-great-great-great-great-grandmother to Jesus.

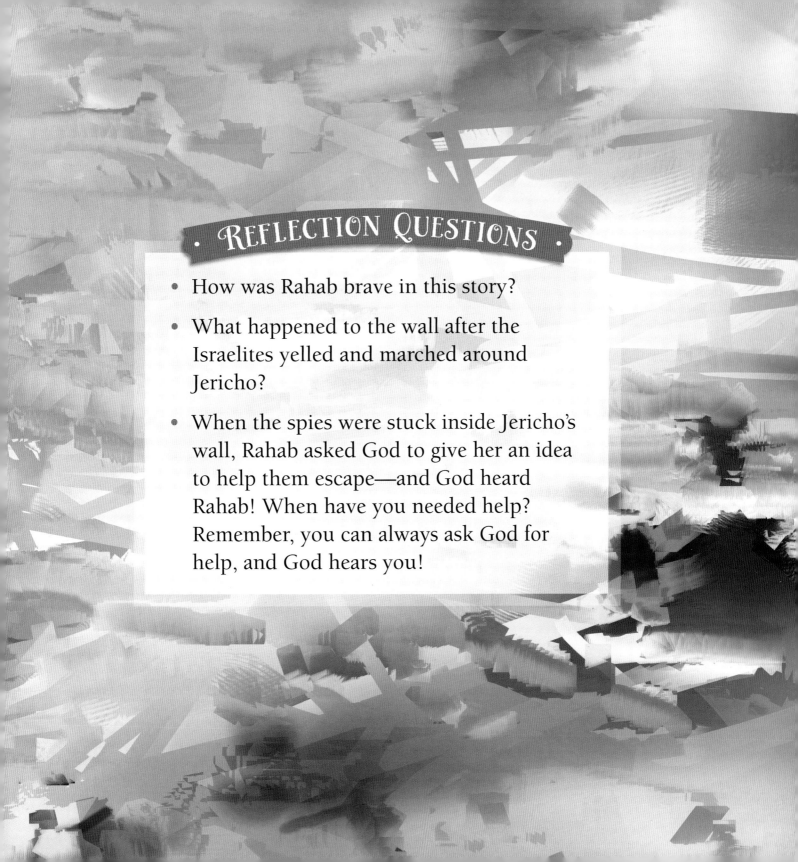

· REFLECTION QUESTIONS ·

- How was Rahab brave in this story?

- What happened to the wall after the Israelites yelled and marched around Jericho?

- When the spies were stuck inside Jericho's wall, Rahab asked God to give her an idea to help them escape—and God heard Rahab! When have you needed help? Remember, you can always ask God for help, and God hears you!

Dear reader,

Rahab's profession may give us pause when we consider sharing her story with our children. Though not traditionally in children's biblical literature, Rahab's story is one to inspire all of us, regardless of our age! Rahab trusted God, risked her life for a nation, and became part of the line of Jesus. Her trust in God was so revolutionary, she was commended twice in the New Testament as an example of faith (Hebrews 11:31; James 2:25). Most of all, hers is a story we can all celebrate—a story of God's redemption and a woman's remarkable courage!

Blessings,

Rachel and Anna

Rachel Spier Weaver is a recruiter at HOPE International and has worked as a career counselor at the University of Florida and Dickinson College. She is passionate about sharing stories of women of God who led in extraordinary ways. She lives with her husband, Shane, and their two children, Norah and Jack.

Anna Haggard is coauthor of *The Spiritual Danger of Doing Good* and *Mission Drift*, a 2015 Christianity Today Book Award winner. A writer and editor for the Brethren in Christ U.S., Anna previously was a staff writer for HOPE International. She is delighted to write for children (her favorite people).

Eric Elwell is a freelance illustrator who blends traditional and digital art techniques. When he's not hanging out in western New York with his beautiful wife and giving piggyback rides to his three children, he enjoys roasting coffee. Connect with him at www.ericelwellart.com